An Honorable Heritage

AN HONORABLE HERITAGE

The Pandita Ramabai Story in Her Own Words

PANDITA RAMABAI

Published by Community Christian Ministries
P.O. Box 9754, Moscow, Idaho 83843
208.883.0997 | www.ccmbooks.org

Pandita Ramabai, *An Honorable Heritage: The Pandita Ramabai Story in Her Own Words.*
Copyright © 1993 by Ramabai Mukti Mission, Clinton, NJ. Used by permission. This book is an adaptation of Pandita Ramabai's autobiograhy, *The High-Caste Hindu Woman*, originally published in 1887.

First CCM edition published 1993. Second edition published in 2019 by Community Christian Ministries.

Cover design by Samuel Dickison.
Interior design by Valerie Anne Bost.

Printed in the United States of America.

Scripture quotations are from the King James Version.

All rights reserved. No part of this publication may be reproduced, stored in a retrieval system, or transmitted in any form by any means, electronic, mechanical, photocopy, recording, or otherwise, without prior permission of the author, except as provided by USA copyright law.

19 20 21 22 23 24 25 26 27   9 8 7 6 5 4 3 2 1

CONTENTS

An Honorable Heritage 1

A Unique Education. 7

Famine, Death and Doubts 15

Introduction to Christianity 21

Calcutta: Deeper Hindu Studies
   and Skepticism. 25

Marriage and Life in Bengal 37

Widowhood and Poona. 41

England: Being Drawn to the Religion
   of Christ 43

Finding Christ	**53**
Telling Others	**69**
Bombay: Founding of Mukti Mission—Home of Salvation	**85**
Glorious New Hope	**93**
Unexpected Visit from the Governor	**97**
A Loving Invitation	**103**
A Note from the Publisher	**107**

AN HONORABLE HERITAGE

MY FATHER, THOUGH A VERY ORTHODOX Hindu and strictly adhering to caste and other religious rules, was yet a reformer in his own way. He could not see why women and people of Shudra[1] caste should not learn to read and write the Sanskrit language and learn sacred literature other than the Vedas.[2]

1 The fourth and lowest of the social classes (castes) in India
2 The most ancient Hindu scriptures

He thought it better to try the experiment at home instead of preaching to others. He found an apt pupil in my mother, who fell in line with his plan, and became an excellent Sanskrit scholar. She performed all her home duties, cooked, washed, and did all household work, took care of her children, attended to guests, and did all that was required of a good religious wife and mother. She devoted many hours of her time in the night to the regular study of the sacred Puranic literature and was able to store up a great deal of knowledge in her mind.

The Brahman Pandits living in the Mangalore District, round about my father's native village, tried to dissuade him from the heretical course he was following in teaching his wife the sacred language of the gods. He had fully prepared himself to

AN HONORABLE HERITAGE

meet their objections. His extensive studies in the Hindu sacred literature enabled him to quote chapter and verse of each sacred book, which gives authority to teach women and Shudras.

His misdeeds were reported to the head priest of the sect to which he belonged, and the learned Brahmans induced the guru to call this heretic to appear before him and before the august assemblage of the Pandits, to give his reasons for taking this course or be excommunicated. He was summoned to Krishnapura and Udipi, the chief seat of the Madhva Vaishnava sect.

My father appeared before the guru, the head priest, and the assembly of Pandits and gave his reasons for teaching his wife. He quoted ancient authorities and succeeded in convincing the guru and chief Pandits that it was not wrong for women and Shudras to learn Sanskrit Puranic literature. So they did not put him out of caste, nor was he molested by anyone after this. He became known as an orthodox reformer.

My father was a native of Mangalore district, but he chose a place in a dense forest on the top of a peak of the Western Ghats, on the borders of Mysore State, where he built a home for himself. This was done in order that he might be away from the hubbub of the world, carry on his educational work, and engage in devotion to the gods in a quiet place, where he would not be constantly worried by curious visitors.

He used to get his support from the rice fields and coconut plantations which he owned. The place he had selected for his home happened to be a sacred place of pilgrimage, where pilgrims came all the year round. He thought it was his duty to entertain them at his expense, as hospitality was a part of his religion. For thirteen years he stayed there and did his work quietly, but lost all his property because of the great expense he incurred in performing what he thought was his duty.

So he was obliged to leave his home and lead a pilgrim's life. My mother told me that I was only about six months old when they left their home. She placed me in a big box made of cane, and a man carried it on his head from the mountain top to the valley. Thus my pilgrim life began when I was a little baby. I was the youngest member of the family.

Some people honoured him for what he was doing, and some despised him.

He cared little for what people said and did what he thought was right. He taught and educated my mother, brother, sister, and others.

A UNIQUE EDUCATION

WHEN I WAS ABOUT EIGHT YEARS OLD, my mother began to teach me and continued to do so until I was about fifteen years of age. During these years, she succeeded in training my mind so that I might be able to carry on my own education with very little aid from others. I did not know of any schools for girls and women existing then where higher education was to be obtained.

Moreover, my parents did not like us children to come in contact with the outside world. They wanted us to be strictly religious and adhere to their old faith. Learning any other language except Sanskrit was out of the question. Secular education of any kind was looked upon as leading people to worldliness which would prevent them from getting into the way of Moksha, or liberation from everlasting trouble of reincarnation in millions and millions of animal species and undergoing the pains of suffering countless millions of diseases and deaths. To learn the English language and to come in contact with the Mlechchhas, as the non-Hindus are called, was forbidden on pain of losing caste and all hope of future happiness. So all that we could or did learn was the Sanskrit grammar and dictionaries, with the

A UNIQUE EDUCATION

Puranic and modern poetical literature in that language. Most of this, including the grammar and dictionaries, which are written in verse form, had to be committed to memory.

Ever since I remember anything, my father and mother were always travelling from one sacred place to another, staying in each place for some months, bathing in the sacred river or tank, visiting temples, worshipping household gods and the images of gods in the temples, and reading Puranas in temples or in some convenient place.

The reading of the Puranas served a double purpose. The first and the foremost was that of getting rid of sin and of earning merit in order to obtain Moksha. The other purpose was to earn an honest living, without begging.

The readers of Puranas—Puranikas as they are called—are the popular and public preachers of religion among the Hindus. They sit in some prominent place, in temple halls or under the trees, or on the banks of rivers and tanks, with their manuscript books in their hands and read the Puranas in a loud voice with intonation, so that the passers-by, or visitors of the temple, might hear.

The text, being in the Sanskrit language, is not understood by the hearers. The Puranikas are not obliged to explain it to them. They may or may not explain it as they choose. And sometimes when it is translated and explained, the Puranika takes great pains to make his speech as popular as he can by telling greatly exaggerated or untrue stories. This is not considered sin, since it is done to attract common people's attention, that they may hear the sacred sound, the names of the gods, and some of their deeds, and be purified by this means.

When the Puranika reads Puranas, the hearers, who are sure to come and sit around him for a few moments at least, generally give him presents. The Puranika continues to read, paying no attention to what the hearers do or say. They come and go at their choice.

When they come, the religious ones among them prostrate themselves before him and worship him and the book, offering flowers, fruits, sweetmeats, garments, money, and other things. It is supposed that this act brings a great deal of merit to the giver, and the person who receives it does not incur any sin. If a hearer does not give presents to the Puranika, he loses all the merit which he may have earned by good acts. The presents need not be very expensive ones: a handful of rice or other grains, a pice, or even a few cowries, which are used as an exchange of pice (64 cowrie shells are equal to one pice), are quite acceptable. A flower, or even a petal of a flower or a leaf of any good sacred tree, is acceptable to the gods. But the offeror knows well that his store of merit will be according to what he gives, and he tries to be as generous as he can. So the Puranika gets all that he needs by reading Puranas in public places.

My parents followed this vocation. We all read Puranas in public places but did not translate or explain them in the vernacular. The reading and hearing of the sacred literature is in itself believed to be productive of great merit—"Punya," as it is called by the Hindus. We never had to beg or work to earn our livelihood. We used to get all the money and food we needed, and more; what remained over after meeting all necessary expenses was spent in performing pilgrimages and giving alms to the Brahmans.

FAMINE, DEATH AND DOUBTS

THIS SORT OF LIFE WENT ON UNTIL MY father became too feeble to stand the exertion, when he was no longer able to direct the reading of the Puranas by us. We were not fit to do any other work to earn our livelihood, as we had grown up in perfect ignorance of anything outside the sacred literature of the Hindus. We could not do menial work, nor could we beg to get the necessities of life.

Our parents had some money in hand. If it had been used to advance our secular education, we might have been able to earn our living in some way. But this was out of the question. Our parents had unbounded faith in what the sacred books said. They encouraged us to look to the gods to get our support. The sacred books declared that if people worshipped the gods in particular ways, gave alms to the Brahmans, repeated the names of certain gods and also some hymns in their honour, with fasting and performance of penance, the gods and goddesses would appear and talk to the worshippers and give them whatever they desired. We decided to take this course of meeting our temporal wants. For three years, we did nothing but perform these religious acts. At last, all the money which we had was spent, but the gods did not help us.

FAMINE, DEATH AND DOUBTS

We suffered from famine which we had brought upon ourselves. The country too, that is, the Madras Presidency where we lived at that particular time, had begun to feel the effects of famine. There was scarcity of food and water. People were starving all around, and we, like the rest of the poor people, wandered from place to place. We were too proud to beg or to do menial work and were ignorant of any practical way of earning an honest living. Nothing but starvation was before us. My father, mother, and sister all died of starvation within a few months of each other.

I cannot describe all the sufferings of that terrible time. My brother and I survived and wandered about, still visiting sacred places, bathing in rivers, and worshipping the gods and goddesses in order to get our desire. We had fulfilled all the conditions laid down in the sacred books and kept all the rules as far as our knowledge went, but the gods were not pleased with us and did not appear to us. After years of fruitless service, we began to lose our faith in them and in the books which prescribed this course and held out the hope of a great reward to the worshippers of the gods. However, we still continued to keep caste rules, worshipped gods, and studied sacred literature as usual.

But as our faith in our religion had grown cold, we were not quite so strict with regard to obtaining secular education and finding some means of earning an honest livelihood. We wandered from place to place, visiting many temples, bathing in many rivers, fasting and performing penances, worshipping gods, trees, animals, Brahmans, and all that

FAMINE, DEATH AND DOUBTS

we knew for more than three years after the death of our parents and elder sister. We had walked more than four thousand miles on foot without any sort of comfort—sometimes eating what kind people gave us, and sometimes going without food, with poor, coarse clothing, and finding but little shelter except in Dharma Shalas, that is, free lodging places for the poor which are common to all pilgrims and travelers of all sorts except the low-caste people. We wandered from the south to the north as far as Kashmir, and then to the east and west to Calcutta in 1878.

INTRODUCTION TO CHRISTIANITY

WE STAYED IN CALCUTTA FOR ABOUT A year and became acquainted with the learned Brahmans. Here my brother and I were once invited to attend a Christian gathering. We did not know what it was, for we had never come in social contact with either the Hindu Reformers, nor with Christians before that time.

We were advised by our Brahman acquaintances to accept this invitation. So we went to the Christian people's gathering for the first time in our lives. We saw many people gathered there who received us very kindly. There were chairs and sofas, tables, lamps—all very new to us. Indian people curiously dressed like English men and women; some men like the Rev. K.M. Banerji and Kali Charan Banerji, whose names sounded like those of Brahmans but whose way of dressing showed that they had become "Sahibs," were great curiosities. They ate bread and biscuits and drank tea with the English people and shocked us by asking us to partake of the refreshment. We thought the last age, Kali Yuga, that is, the age of quarrels, darkness, and irreligion, had fully established its reign in Calcutta

INTRODUCTION TO CHRISTIANITY

since some of the Brahmans were so irreligious as to eat food with the English.

We looked upon the proceedings of the assembly with curiosity but did not understand what they were about. After a little while one of them opened a book and read something out of it, and then they knelt down before their chairs and some said something with closed eyes. We were told that was the way they prayed to God. We did not see any image to which they paid their homage, but it seemed as though they were paying homage to the chairs before which they knelt. Such was the crude idea of Christian worship that impressed itself on my mind.

The kind Christians gave me a copy of the Holy Bible in Sanskrit and some other nice things with it. Two of those people were the translators of the Bible. They were grand old men. I do not remember their names, but they must have prayed for my conversion through the reading of the Bible. I liked the outward appearance of the Book and tried to read it but did not understand. The language was so different from the Sanskrit literature of the Hindus, the teaching so different, that I thought it quite a waste of time to read that Book, but I have never parted with it since then.

CALCUTTA

Deeper Hindu Studies and Skepticism

WHILE STAYING IN CALCUTTA WE became acquainted with many learned Pandits. Some of them requested me to lecture to the Pardah[3] women on the duties of women according to the Shastras. I had to study the subject well before I

3 The practice of secluding women from public view by concealing clothing such as veils and by enclosures and screens within the home

could lecture on it, so I bought the books of the Hindu law published in Calcutta. Besides reading them, I read other books which would help me in my work. While reading the Dharma Shastras, I came to know many things which I never knew before. There were contradictory statements about almost everything. What one book said was most righteous, the other book declared as being unrighteous. While reading the Mahabharata I found the following: "The Vedas differ from each other; Smrities, that is, books of sacred laws, do not agree with one another; the secret of religion is in some hidden place. The only way is that which is followed by great men."

This I found true of about everything, but there were two things on which all those books, the Dharma Shastras, the sacred epics, the Puranas and modern poets, the popular preachers of the present day and orthodox high-caste men were agreed: women of high and low caste, as a class, were bad, very bad, worse than demons, and they could not get Moksha as men. The only hope of their getting this much-desired liberation from Karma and its results, that is, countless millions of births and deaths and untold suffering, was the worship of their husbands. The husband is said to be the woman's god; there is no other god for her. This god may be the worst sinner and a great criminal; still HE IS HER GOD, and she must worship him. She can have no hope of getting admission into Svarga, the abode of the gods, without his pleasure; and if she pleases him in all things, she will have the privilege of going to Svarga as his slave, there to serve him and be one of his wives among the thousands of the Svarga harlots who are presented to him by the gods in exchange for his wife's merit.

The woman is allowed to go into higher existence thus far but to attain Moksha or liberation, she must perform such great religious acts as will obtain for her the merit by which she will be reincarnated as a high caste man, in order to study Vedas and the Vedanta, and thereby get the knowledge of the true Brahma and be amalgamated in it. The extraordinary religious acts which help a woman to get into the way of getting Moksha are utter abandonment of her will to that of her husband. She is to worship him with whole-hearted devotion as the only god, to know and see no other pleasure in life except in the most degraded slavery to him. The woman has no right to study the Vedas and Vedanta, and without knowing them, no one can know the Brahma. Without knowing Brahma, no one can get liberation; therefore, no woman as a woman can get liberation, that is, Moksha. Q.E.D.

The same rules are applicable to the Shudras. The Shudras must not study the Veda and must not perform the same religious acts which a Brahman[4] has a right to perform. The Shudra who hears the Veda repeated must be punished by having his ears filled with liquefied lead. The Shudra who dares to learn a verse or verses of the Veda must be punished by having intensely hot liquor poured down his throat. This would no doubt be done

4 A member of the highest, or priestly, caste

to the Shudra who violates the sacred law, if he were left to the tender mercies of the Brahman. His only hope of getting liberation is in serving the three high castes as their lifelong slave. Then he will earn merit enough to be reincarnated in some higher caste, and in the course of millions of years, he will be born as a Brahman, learn the Vedas and Vedantas, and get knowledge of the Brahma and be amalgamated in it. Such is the hope of final liberation held out by the Shastras to women and to the Shudras.

As for the low-caste people,[5] the poor things have no hope of any sort. They are looked upon as being very like the lower species of animals, such as pigs; their very shadow and the sound of their voices are defiling; they have no place in the abode

---

5 The "untouchables"

of the gods and no hope of getting liberation, except that they might perchance be born among the higher castes after having gone through millions of reincarnations.

The things which are necessary to make it possible for them to be born in higher castes are that they should be contented to live in a very degraded condition, serving the high-caste people as their bondservants, eating the leavings of their food in dirty broken earthen vessels, wearing filthy rags and clothes thrown away from the dead bodies of the high-caste people. They may sometimes get the benefit of coming in contact with the shadow of a Brahman and have a few drops of water from his hand or wet clothes thrown at them and feel the air which has passed over the sacred persons of Brahmans. These things are beneficial to the low-caste people, but the Brahmans lose much of their own hard-earned merit by letting the low-caste people get these benefits!

The low-caste people are never allowed to enter the temples where high-caste men worship gods. So the poor degraded people find shapeless stones and broken pots, smear them with red paint, set them up under trees and on road sides, or in small temples which they build themselves, where Brahmans do not go for fear of losing their caste, and worship, in order to satisfy the cravings of their spiritual nature. Poor, poor people! How very sad their condition is no one who has not seen can realize. Their quarters are found outside every village or town where the sacred feet of the pious Brahmans do not walk!

These are the two things upon which all Shastras and others are agreed. I had a vague idea of these doctrines of the Hindu religion from my childhood, but while studying the Dharma Shastras, they presented themselves to my mind with great force. My eyes were being gradually opened; I was waking up to my own hopeless condition as a woman, and it was becoming clearer and clearer to me that I had no place anywhere as far as religious consolation was concerned. I became quite dissatisfied with myself. I wanted something more than the Shastras could give me, but I did not know what it was that I wanted.

One day my brother and I were invited by Keshab Chandra Sen to his house. He received us very kindly, took me into the inner part of the house, and introduced me to his wife and daughters. One of them was just married to the Maharaja of Cuch Behar, and the Brahmos[6] and others were criticising him for breaking the rule which was laid down for all Brahmos, that is, not to marry or give girls in marriage under fourteen years of age.

He and his family showed great kindness to me, and when parting, he gave me a copy of one of the Vedas. He asked if I had studied the Vedas. I answered in the negative, and said that women were not fit to read the Vedas, and they were not

---

6 From https://www.britannica.com/topic/Brahmo-Samaj: A "theistic movement within Hinduism, founded in Calcutta in 1828 by Ram Mohun Roy. The Brahmo Samaj does not accept the authority of the Vedas, has no faith in avatars (incarnations), and does not insist on belief in karma (causal effects of past deeds) or samsara (the process of death and rebirth).... Influenced by Islam and Christianity, it denounces polytheism, image worship, and the caste system."

allowed to do so. It would be breaking the rules of religion if I were to study the Vedas. He could not but smile at my declaration of this Hindu doctrine. He said nothing in answer, but advised me to study the Vedas and Upanishads.

New thoughts were awakening in my heart. I questioned myself as to why I should not study Vedas and Vedanta. Soon I persuaded myself into the belief that it was not wrong for a woman to read the Vedas. So I began first to read the Upanishads, then the Vedanta, and the Veda. I became more dissatisfied with myself.

In the meanwhile, my brother died. As my father wanted me to be well-versed in our religion, he did not give me in marriage when a little child. He had married my older sister to a boy of her own age, but he did not want to study or to lead a good religious life with my sister. Her life was made miserable by being unequally yoked, and my father did not want the same thing to happen to me. This was of course against the caste rules, so he had to suffer, being practically put out of Brahman society. But he stood the persecution with his characteristic manliness and did what he thought was right, to give me a chance to study and be happy by leading a religious life. So I had remained unmarried till I was 22 years old.

Having lost all faith in the religion of my ancestors, I married a Bengali gentleman of the Shudra caste. My husband died of cholera within two years of our marriage, and I was left alone to face the world with one baby in my arms.

MARRIAGE AND LIFE IN BENGAL

I STAYED IN BENGAL AND ASSAM FOR four years in all and studied the Bengali language. While living with my husband at Silchar, Assam, I had found a little pamphlet in my library. I do not know how it came there, but I picked it up and began to read it with great interest. It was St. Luke's Gospel in the Bengali language.

There was a Baptist missionary, Mr. Allen, living at Silchar. He occasionally paid visits to me and preached the gospel. He explained the first chapter of the Book of Genesis to me. The story of the creation of the world was so very unlike all the stories which I read in the Puranas and Shastras that I became greatly interested in it. It struck me as being a true story, but I could not give any reason for thinking so or believing in it.

Having lost all faith in my former religion, and with my heart hungering after something better, I eagerly learnt everything which I could about the Christian religion and declared my intention to become a Christian if I were perfectly satisfied with this new religion. My husband, who had studied in a mission school, was pretty well acquainted with the Bible but did not like to be called a Christian. Much less did he like the idea of his wife being publicly baptized and joining the despised Christian community. He was very angry and said he would tell Mr. Allen not to come to our house any more. I do not know just what would have happened had he lived much longer.

I was desperately in need of some religion. The Hindu religion held out no hope for me; the Brahmo religion was not a very definite one. For it is nothing but what a man makes for himself. He chooses and gathers whatever seems good to him from all religions known to him and prepares a sort of religion for his own use. The Brahmo religion has no other foundation than man's own natural light and the sense of right and wrong which he possesses in common with all mankind. It could not and did not satisfy me; still I liked and believed a good deal of it that was better than what the orthodox Hindu religion taught.

WIDOWHOOD AND POONA

AFTER MY HUSBAND'S DEATH, I LEFT Silchar and came to Poona. Here I stayed for a year. The leaders of the reform party and the members of the Prarthana Samaj[7] treated me with great kindness and gave me some help. Messrs. Ranade, Modak, Kelkar and Dr. Bhandarkar were among the people who showed great kindness to me. Miss Hurford, then a missionary

---

7 A Hindu reform society similar to the Brahmo

working in connection with the High Church, used to come and teach me the New Testament in Marathi. I had at this time begun to study the English language but did not know how to write or speak it. She used to teach me some lessons from the primary reading books, yet sometimes I was more interested in the study of the New Testament than in the reading books. The Rev. Father Goreh was another missionary who used to come and explain the difference between the Hindu and Christian religions. I profited much by their teaching.

ENGLAND

*Being Drawn to
the Religion of Christ*

I WENT TO ENGLAND EARLY IN 1883 IN order to study and fit myself for my life-work. When I first landed in England, I was met by the kind Sisters of Wantage, one of whom I had been introduced to by Miss Hurford at St. Mary's Home in Poona. The Sisters took me to their home, and one of them, who became my spiritual mother, began to teach me both secular and religious subjects. I owe an everlasting debt of gratitude to her, and to Miss Beale, the late Lady Principal of Cheltenham Ladies' College. Both of these ladies took great pains with me and taught me the subjects which would help me in my life work. The instruction which I received from them was mostly spiritual. Their motherly kindness and deeply spiritual influence have greatly helped in building up my character. I praise and thank God for permitting me to be under the loving Christian care of these ladies.

The Mother Superior once sent me for a change to one of the branches of the Sisters' Home in London. The Sisters there took me to see the rescue work carried on by them. I met several of the women who had once been in their Rescue Home, but who had so completely changed and were so filled with the love of Christ and compassion for suffering humanity, that they had given their life for the service of the sick and infirm. Here for the first time in my life I came to know that something should be done to reclaim the so-called fallen women, and that Christians, whom Hindus considered outcastes and cruel, were kind to these unfortunate women, degraded in the eyes of society.

I had never heard or seen anything of the kind done for this class of women by the Hindus in my own country. I had not heard anyone speaking kindly of them, nor seen any one making any effort to turn them from the evil path they had chosen in their folly. The Hindu Shastras do not deal kindly with these women. The law of the Hindu commands that the king shall cause the fallen women to be eaten by dogs in the outskirts of the town. They are considered the greatest sinners and not worthy of compassion.

After my visit to the Homes at Fulham, where I saw the work of mercy carried on by the Sisters of the Cross, I began to think that there was a real difference between Hinduism and Christianity. I asked the Sisters who instructed me to tell me what it was that made the Christians care for and reclaim the "fallen" women. She read the story of Christ meeting the Samaritan woman and His wonderful discourse on the nature of true worship, and explained it to me. She spoke of the infinite love of Christ for sinners. He did not despise them but came to save them.

I had never read or heard anything like this in the religious books of the Hindus;

I realized, after reading the 4th chapter of St. John's Gospel, that Christ was truly the Divine Saviour He claimed to be, and no one but He could transform and uplift the downtrodden womanhood of India and of every land.

Thus my heart was drawn to the religion of Christ. I was intellectually convinced of its truth on reading a book written by Father Goreh and was baptized in the Church of England in the latter part of 1883, while living with the Sisters at Wantage. I was comparatively happy and felt a great joy in finding a new religion which was better than any other religion I had known before. I knew full well that it would displease my friends and my countrymen very much, but I have never regretted having taken the step. I was hungry for something better than what the Hindu Shastras gave. I found it in the Christian's Bible and was satisfied.

After my baptism and confirmation, I studied the Christian religion more thoroughly with the help of various books written on its doctrines. I was much confused by finding so many different teachings of different sects, each one giving the authority of the Bible for holding a special doctrine, and for differing from other sects.

For five years after my baptism I studied these different doctrines and made close observations during my stay in England and in America. Besides meeting people of the most prominent sects, the High Church, Low Church, Baptist, Methodist, Presbyterian, Friends, Unitarian, Universalist, Roman Catholic, Jews, and others, I met with Spiritualists,

Theosophists, Mormons, Christian Scientists, and followers of what they call the occult religion.

No one can have any idea of what my feelings were at finding such a Babel of religions in Christian countries, and at finding how very different the teaching of each sect was from that of the others. I recognized the Nastikas of India in the Theosophists, the polygamous Hindu in the Mormons, the worshippers of ghosts and demons in the Spiritualists, and the Old Vedantists in the Christian Scientists. Their teachings were not new to me. I had known them in their old eastern nature as they are in India; and, when I met them in America, I thought they had only changed their Indian dress and put on Western garbs, which were more suitable to the climate and conditions of the country.

As for the differences of the orthodox and non-orthodox Christian sects, I could not account for them, except that I thought it must be in the human nature to have them. The differences did not seem of any more importance than those existing among the different sects of Brahmanical Hindu religion. They only showed that people were quarrelling with each other, and there was no oneness of mind in them.

Although I was quite contented with my newly-found religion, so far as I understood it, still I was labouring under great intellectual difficulties, and my heart longed for something better which I had not found. I came to know after eight years from the time of my baptism that I had found the Christian religion, which was good enough for me; but I had not found Christ, Who is the Life of the religion and "the Light of every man that cometh into the world."

FINDING CHRIST

IT WAS NOBODY'S FAULT THAT I HAD not found Christ. He must have been preached to me from the beginning. My mind at that time had been too dull to grasp the teaching of the Holy Scriptures. The open Bible had been before me, but I had given much of my time to the study of other books about the Bible and had not studied the Bible itself as I should have done: hence my ignorance of many important doctrines taught in it. I gave up the study of other books about the Bible after my return home from America and took to reading the Bible regularly.

Following this course for about two years, I became very unhappy in my mind. I was dissatisfied with my spiritual condition. One day I went to the Bombay Guardian Mission Press on some business. There I picked up a book called *From Death unto Life*, written by Mr. Haslam, the evangelist. I read his experiences in this book with great interest. He, being a clergyman of the Church of England, had charge of a good parish and was interested in all Christian activities connected with the Church. While he was holding conversation with a lady, a member of his Church, she told him that he was trying to build from the top. The

FINDING CHRIST

lady meant to say he was not converted and had not experienced regeneration and salvation in Christ.

I read his account of his conversion and work for Christ. Then I began to consider where I stood, and what my actual need was. I took the Bible and read portions of it, meditating on the messages which God gave me. There were so many things I did not understand intellectually. One thing I knew by this time: I needed Christ and not merely His religion.

There were some of the old ideas stamped on my brain; for instance, I thought that repentance of sin and the determination to give it up was what was necessary for forgiveness of sin: that the rite of baptism was the means of regeneration; that my sins were truly washed away when I was baptized in the name of Christ. These and such other ideas, which are akin to Hindu mode of religious thought, stuck to me. For some years after my baptism, I was comparatively happy to think that I had found a religion which gave its privileges equally to men and women; there was no distinction of caste, colour, or sex made in it.

All this was very beautiful, no doubt. But I had failed to understand that we are of "God in Christ Jesus, who of God is made unto us wisdom, and righteousness, and sanctification and redemption" (1 Cor. 1:30). I had failed to see the need of placing my implicit faith in Christ and His atonement in order to become a child of God by being born again of the Holy Spirit and justified by faith in the Son of God. My thoughts were not very clear on this and other points. I was desperate. I realised that I was not prepared to meet God, that sin had dominion over me, and I was not altogether led by the Spirit of God and had not therefore received the Spirit of adoption and had no witness of the Spirit that I was a child of God. "For as many as are led by the Spirit of God, they are the sons of God. For ye have not received the spirit of bondage again to fear; but ye have received the Spirit of adoption whereby we cry, 'Abba, Father.' The Spirit itself beareth witness with our spirit, that we are the children of God" (Rom. 8:14–16).

What was to be done? My thoughts could not and did not help me. I had at last come to an end of myself and unconditionally surrendered myself to the Saviour; and asked Him to be merciful to me, and to become my Righteousness and Redemption, and to take away all my sin.

Only those who have been convicted of sin and have seen themselves as God sees them under similar circumstances can understand what one feels when a great and unbearable burden is rolled away from one's heart. I shall not attempt to describe how and what I felt at the time when I made an unconditional surrender and knew I was accepted to be a branch of the True Vine, a child of God by adoption in Christ Jesus my Saviour.

Although it is impossible for me to tell all that God has done for me, I must yet praise Him and thank Him for His lovingkindness to me, the greatest of sinners. The Lord, first of all, showed me the sinfulness of sin and the awful danger I was in of everlasting hell-fire and the great love of God with which He "so loved the world, that He gave His only begotten

FINDING CHRIST 59

Son" (John 3:16). And He gave this Son to be the propitiation for my sin: for does not the inspired Apostle say, "We have an Advocate with the Father, Jesus Christ the Righteous: and He is the Propitiation for our sins: and not for ours only but also for the sins of the whole world" (1 John 2:1–2).

The Bible says that God does not wait for me to merit His love but heaps it upon me without my deserving it. It says also that there is neither male nor female in Christ. "The righteousness of God which is by faith of Jesus Christ, unto all and upon all them that believe: for there is no difference: for all have sinned, and come short of the glory of God; being justified freely by His grace through the redemption that is in Christ Jesus: Whom God hath set forth to be a propitiation through faith in His blood to declare His righteousness for the remission of sins that are past, through the forbearance of God; to declare I say at this time His righteousness: that He might be just, and the justifier of him which believeth in Jesus" (Rom. 3:22–26).

I do not know if any one of my readers has ever had the experience of being shut up in a room where there was nothing but thick darkness and then groping in it to find something of which he or she was in dire need. I can think of no one but the blind man, whose story is given in St. John chapter nine. He was born blind and remained so for forty years of his life; and then suddenly he found the Mighty One Who could give him eyesight. Who could have described his joy at seeing the daylight, when there had not been a particle of hope of his ever seeing it? Even the inspired evangelist has not attempted to do it. I can give only a faint idea of what I felt when my mental eyes were opened, and when I who was "sitting in darkness saw Great Light," and when I felt sure that to me, who but a few moments ago "sat in the region and shadow of death, light had sprung up" (Matt. 4:16). I was very like the man who was told, "In the name of Jesus Christ of Nazareth rise up and walk . . . . And he leaping up stood, and walked, and entered with them into the temple, walking and leaping and praising God" (Acts 3:6, 8).

I looked to the blessed Son of God who was lifted up on the cross and there suffered death, even the death of the cross, in my stead, that I might be made free from the bondage of sin and from the fear of death, and I received life. O the love, the unspeakable love of the Father for me, a lost sinner, which gave His only Son to die for me! I had not merited this love, but that was the very reason why He showed it to me.

How very different the truth of God was from the false idea that I had entertained from my earliest childhood. That was that I must have merit to earn present or future happiness, the pleasure of Svarga, or face the utterly inconceivable loss of Moksha or liberation. This I could never hope for, since a woman, as a woman, has no hope of Moksha according to Hindu religion. The Brahman priests have tried to deceive the women and the Shudras and other low-caste people into the belief that they have some hope. But when we study for ourselves the books of the religious law and enquire from the higher authorities,

FINDING CHRIST

we find that there is nothing, no, nothing whatever for us.

They say that women and Shudras and other low-caste people can gain Svarga by serving the husband and the Brahman. But the happiness of Svarga does not last long. The final blessed state to which the Brahman is entitled is not for women and low-caste people. But here this blessed Book, the Christians' Bible, says:

> When we were yet without strength, in due time Christ died for the ungodly. For scarcely for a righteous man will one die: yet peradventure for a good man some would even dare to die. But God commendeth His love toward us, in that, while we were yet sinners Christ died for us.... For...

> when we were enemies, we were reconciled to God by the death of His Son. (Rom. 5:6–10)

> In this was manifested the love of God toward us, because that God sent His only begotten Son into the world, that we might live through Him. Herein is love, not that we loved God, but that He loved us, and sent His Son to be the propitiation for our sins. (1 John 4:9–10)

How good, how indescribably good! What good news for me a woman, a woman born in India among Brahmans who hold out no hope for me and the like of me! The Bible declares that Christ did not reserve this great salvation for a particular caste or sex.

> But as many as received Him, to them gave He power to become the sons of God, even to them that believe on His name: which were born, not of blood, nor of the will of the flesh, nor of the will of man, but of God. (John 1:12–13)

> For the grace of God that bringeth salvation hath appeared to all men. (Titus 2:11)

> The kindness and love of God our Saviour toward man appeared, not by works of righteousness which we have done, but according to His mercy He saved us. (Titus 3:4)

No caste, no sex, no work, and no man was to be depended upon to get salvation, this everlasting life, but God gave it freely to anyone and everyone who believed on His Son Whom He sent to be the "propitiation for our sins." And there was not a particle of doubt left as to whether this salvation was a present one or not. I had not to wait till after undergoing births and deaths for countless millions of times, when I should become a Brahman man, in order to get to know the Brahma. And then, was there any joy and happiness to be hoped for? No, there is nothing but to be amalgamated into Nothingness-Shunya, Brahma.

> The Son of God says, "Verily, verily, I say unto you He that heareth my word, and believeth on Him that sent me hath everlasting life, and shall not come into

condemnation but is passed from death to life" (John 5:24).

If we receive the witness of men, the witness of God is greater; for this is the witness of God which He hath testified of His Son. He that believeth on the Son of God hath the witness in himself: he that believeth not God, hath made Him a liar: because he believeth not the record that God gave of His Son. And this is the record, that *God hath given to us eternal life, and this life is in His Son.* He that hath the Son hath life; and he that hath not the Son of God hath not life. These things have I written unto you that believe on the name of the Son of God; that ye may know that ye have eternal life and that ye may believe on the name of the Son of God. (1 John 5:9–13)

The Holy Spirit made it clear to me from the Word of God, that the salvation which God gives through Christ is present, and not something future. I believed it; I received it; and I was filled with joy.

TELLING OTHERS

SIXTEEN YEARS AGO, A NEW LEAF WAS turned in my life. Since then I have come to know the Lord Jesus Christ as my personal Saviour and have the joy of sweet communion with Him. My life is full of joy, "For the Lord Jehovah is my strength and my song; He also is become my salvation" (Isa. 12:2). Now I know what the Prophet means by saying, "Therefore with joy shall ye draw water out of the wells of salvation" (Isa. 12:3). I can scarcely contain the joy and keep it to myself. I feel like the Samaritan woman who "left her waterpot, and went her way into the city, and saith to the men, Come, see a man, which told me all things that ever I did: is not this the Christ?" (John 4:29).

I feel I must tell my fellow creatures what great things the Lord Jesus has done for me, and I feel sure, as it was possible for Him to save such a great sinner as I am, He is quite able to save others. The only thing that must be done by me is to tell people of Him and of His love for sinners and His great power to save them.

My readers will not therefore find fault with me for making this subject so very personal. The heart-experiences of an individual are too sacred to be exposed to the public gaze. Why then should I give them to the public in this way? Because a "necessity is laid upon me; yea, woe is unto me, if I preach not the gospel!" (1 Cor. 9:16). I am bound to tell as many men and women as possible that Christ Jesus came to save sinners like me. He has saved me, praise the Lord! I know "He is able also to save them to the uttermost that come unto God by Him, seeing He ever liveth to make intercession for them" (Heb. 7:25).

God has given me a practical turn of mind. I wanted to find out the truth about everything including religion by experiment. I experimented on the religion in which I was born. I did not leave a stone unturned, as it were, as far as I knew; not only in the way of studying books, but of doing myself what the books prescribed. I have seen many others also doing the same thing. I saw them doing everything that was commanded them. The sad end was that I found that they were not saved by it, nor was I. It was a dire spiritual necessity that drove me to seek help from other sources. I had to give up all pride of our ancestral religion being old and superior, which is preventing many of my country-people from finding Christ, although they know well that they have not got the joy of salvation. They can never have it except in Christ.

There are I know many hungry souls, and maybe some of them might be helped by reading this account. I would urge upon such brothers and sisters to make haste and come forward and accept the great love of God expressed in Christ Jesus and not to neglect "so great salvation," which God gives freely (Heb. 2:1–3).

"Neither is there salvation in any other: for there is none other name under heaven given among men, whereby we must be saved" (Acts 4:12).

Do not therefore lose time through pride or because of any other difficulty. The caste may put you out; your near and dear ones will perhaps reject you and persecute you. You may very likely lose your temporal greatness, and riches; but never mind, the great salvation which you will get in Christ by believing on Him and confessing Him before men is worth all the great sacrifices you can possibly make. Yes, and more than that, for all the riches and all the gain, and all the joys of the world, do not begin to compare with the joy *of salvation.*

On the other hand, of what use are all the riches and greatness of the world, if you are condemned to the second death and are to live in the lake of fire forever and ever suffering indescribable agonies from which there is no relief? "For what shall it profit a man, if he shall gain the whole world and lose his own soul? Or what shall a man give in exchange for his soul?" (Mark 8:36–37).

I would urge on you, dear brother and sister, to make haste and get reconciled with God through Christ. For the great day of judgment is fast coming on us, so make haste and flee from the wrath of God, which you and I have justly merited. God is Love, and He is waiting patiently for you to accept His great salvation, so despise not "the riches of His goodness and forbearance and longsuffering," and know "that the goodness of God leadeth thee to repentance" (Rom. 2:4).

TELLING OTHERS

I found it a great blessing to realize the personal presence of the Holy Spirit in me and to be guided and taught by Him. I have experienced the sweet pleasure promised by the Lord in Psalm 32:8, "I will instruct thee and teach thee in the way which thou shalt go: I will guide thee with mine eye."

The Holy Spirit taught me how to appropriate every promise of God in the right way and obey His voice. I am sorry to say that I have failed to obey Him many a time, but He tenderly rebukes and shows me my faults. Many a time He finds it most necessary to punish me in various ways. His promise is: "I will correct thee in measure, and will not leave thee altogether unpunished" (Jer. 30:11).

I have many failures and am corrected as the Lord sees fit. It is always helpful to be shown that His hand is in everything that happens. Then no room is left for murmuring. Whenever I heed and obey the Lord's voice with all my heart, I am very happy and everything goes right. Even the tests of faith and difficulties and afflictions become great blessings.

Since the year 1891, I have tried to witness for Christ in my weakness, and I have always found that it is the greatest joy of the Christian life to tell people of Christ and of His great love for sinners.

About twelve years ago, I read the inspiring books, *The Story of the China Inland Mission*, *The Lord's Dealings with George Müller*, and the *Life of John G. Paton*, founder of the New Hebrides Mission. I was greatly impressed with the experiences of these three great men, Mr. Hudson Taylor, Mr. Müller and Mr. Paton, all of whom have gone to be with the Lord within a few years of each other. I wondered after reading their lives if it were not possible to trust the Lord in India as in other countries. I wished very much that there were some missions founded in this country, which would be a testimony to the Lord's faithfulness to His people and the truthfulness of what the Bible says, in a practical way.

I questioned in my mind over and over again, why some missionaries did not come forward to found faith missions in India. Then the Lord said to me, "Why don't *you* begin to do this yourself, instead of wishing for others to do it? How easy it is for anyone to wish that someone else would do a difficult thing, instead of doing it himself." I was greatly rebuked by the "Still Small Voice" which spoke to me.

I did not know then that there were some faith missions in India. Since then I have come to know that there are a few faith missions working in this country, and I thank God for setting them up here and there, as great beacon lights.

At the end of 1896 when the great famine came on this country, I was led by the Lord to step forward and start new work, trusting Him for both temporal and spiritual blessings. I can testify with all my heart that I have always found the Lord faithful. "Faithful is He that calleth you" (1 Thess. 5:24). This golden text has been written with the life-blood of Christ on my heart. The Lord has done countless great things for me. I do not deserve His lovingkindness. I can testify to the truth of Psalm 103:10, "He hath not dealt with us after our sins; nor rewarded us according to our iniquities."

TELLING OTHERS

Here are some of the things which the Lord has been teaching me during the past sixteen years, especially in the last decade since He brought this Mukti Mission into existence:

> Men have not heard, nor perceived by the ear, neither hath the eye seen, O God, beside Thee, what He hath prepared for him that waiteth for Him. (Isa. 64:4)
>
> All the promises of God in Him are yea, and in Him Amen, unto the glory of God by us. (2 Cor. 1:20)
>
> The gifts and calling of God are without repentance. (Rom. 11:29)
>
> My unbelief shall not "make the faith of God without effect" (Rom. 3:3).

> The secret of the Lord is with them that fear Him; and He will shew them His covenant. (Ps. 25:14)
>
> The blood of Jesus Christ His Son cleanseth us from all sin. (1 John 1:7)
>
> This is a faithful saying, and worthy of all acceptation, that Christ Jesus came into the world to save sinners; of whom I am chief. (1 Tim. 1:15)

In short, the Lord has been teaching me His Word by His Spirit and unfolding the wonders of His works, day by day. I have come to believe the Word of God implicitly, and I have found out by experience, that *it is true.* I praise God and thank Him for His mercies to me and mine. Hallelujah!

I feel very happy since the Lord called me to step out in faith, and I obeyed. To depend upon Him for everything; for spiritual life, for bodily health, for advice, for food, water, clothing, and all other necessities of life, in short, to realise by experiment, that the promises of God in Philippians 4:6, 19, and in other parts of the Holy Scriptures are true, is most blessed.

> Be careful for nothing; but in everything by prayer and supplication with thanksgiving, let your requests be made known unto God. (Phil. 4:6)
>
> And my God will supply every need of yours according to his riches in glory in Christ Jesus. (Phil. 4:19)

> I am the Lord thy God, which brought thee out of the land of Egypt: open thy mouth wide, and I will fill it. (Ps. 81:10)

> It is better to trust in the Lord than to put confidence in man. It is better to trust in the Lord than to put confidence in princes. (Ps. 118:8–9)

I am spared all trouble and care, casting my burden upon the Lord. There are over 1,500 people living here. We are not rich, nor great, but we are happy, getting our daily bread directly from the loving hands of our Heavenly Father, having not a piece over and above our daily necessities, having no banking account anywhere, no endowment or income from any earthly source, but depending

TELLING OTHERS

altogether on our Father God; we have nothing to fear from anybody, nothing to lose, and nothing to regret. The Lord is our Inexhaustible Treasure.

"The Eternal God is thy refuge, and underneath are the everlasting arms" (Deut. 33:27). We are confidently resting in His arms, and He is loving and faithful in all His dealings with us. How can I express in words the gratitude I feel toward such a Father, and the joy that fills my heart because of His goodness?

> Bless the Lord, O my soul, and all that is within me bless His holy name. Bless the Lord, O my soul, and forget not all His benefits: Who forgiveth all thine iniquities; Who healeth all thy diseases; Who redeemeth thy life from

destruction; Who crowneth thee with loving-kindness and tender mercies; Who satisfieth thy mouth with good things; so that thy youth is renewed like the eagle's. (Ps. 103:1–5)

BOMBAY

Founding of Mukti Mission— Home of Salvation

NINETEEN YEARS AGO, IN THIS MONTH of July, I started from the city of Philadelphia and went to San Francisco, in response to the kind invitation sent by some good friends who took a deep interest in the well-being of the women of India. I lived in the latter city for more than four months and sailed from the Golden Gate for Bombay, via Japan and China.

God in His great goodness gave me faithful and true friends in America who promised to help me in my work. My work, in the beginning, was a purely educational one, and religious liberty was to be given to the inmates of my school, and all plans were made to start the Home for Widows as soon as I should land in Bombay.

The day for sailing from San Francisco arrived. I felt as if I were going to a strange country and to a strange people. Everything seemed quite dark before me. I fell on my knees, committed myself to the care of our loving Heavenly Father, and sailed.

My religious belief was so vague at the time that I was not certain whether I would go to heaven or hell after my death.

I was not prepared to meet my God then. How can I describe my feelings when I heard of the disaster at San Francisco by the terrible earthquake, and of the great destruction of human life in the harbour of Hong Kong not long ago? How I thanked God for letting me live all these years and not sending the terrible earthquake and the dreadful storms when I was not prepared to meet Him. I deeply sympathise with the people living in both of these places in their afflictions and pray to God that He may save each and all of the surviving inhabitants of San Francisco and Hong Kong.

When starting from San Francisco, and on landing in Bombay, I had resolved in my mind that although no direct religious instruction was to be given to the inmates of my home, yet I would daily read the

Bible aloud and pray to the only True God in the name of Christ; that my countrywomen, seeing and hearing what was going on, might be led to enquire about the true religion and the way of salvation.

There were only two day-pupils in my school when it was started a little more than eighteen years ago. No one was urged to become a Christian, nor was anyone compelled to study the Bible. But the Book was placed in the library along with other religious books. The daily testimony to the goodness of the True God awakened new thoughts in many a heart.

After the first ten years of our existence as a school, our constitution was changed slightly. Since then, every pupil admitted in the school has been receiving religious instruction, retaining perfect liberty of conscience.

Many hundreds of the girls and young women who have come to my Home ever since its doors were opened for them have found Christ as I have. They are capable of thinking for themselves. They have had their eyes opened by reading the Word of God, and many of them have been truly converted and saved to the praise and glory of God. I thank God for letting me see several hundred of my sisters, the children of my love and prayer, gloriously saved. All this was done by God in answer to the prayers of faith of thousands of His faithful servants in all lands, who are constantly praying for us all.

I was led by the Lord to start a special prayer circle at the beginning of 1905. There were about seventy of us who met together each morning and prayed for the true conversion of all the Indian

Christians including ourselves, and for a special outpouring of the Holy Spirit on all Christians of every land. In six months from the time we began to pray in this manner, the Lord graciously sent a glorious Holy Ghost revival among us, and also in many schools and churches in this country. The results of this have been most satisfactory. Many hundreds of our girls and some of our boys have been gloriously saved, and many of them are serving God and witnessing for Christ at home and in other places.

I have responded to the Lord's challenge, "Prove Me now" (Mal. 3:10), and have found Him faithful and true. I know He is a prayer-hearing and prayer-answering God. His promise, "My people shall never be ashamed" (Joel 2:16), and all the thousands of His promises are true. I entreat you, my readers, to prove the Lord as I have proved Him.

> O taste and see that the Lord is good; blessed is the man that trusteth in Him. O fear the Lord, ye His saints; for there is no want to them that fear Him. The young lions do lack, and suffer hunger: but they that seek the Lord shall not want any good thing. (Ps. 34:8–10)

> O give thanks unto the Lord for He is good: for His mercy endureth for ever. Let the redeemed of the Lord say so, whom He hath redeemed from the hand of the enemy: And gathered them out of the lands, from the east and from the west, from the north, and

> from the south. They wandered in the wilderness in a solitary way; they found no city to dwell in. Hungry and thirsty, their soul fainted in them. Then they cried unto the Lord in their trouble, and He delivered them out of their distresses. And He led them forth by the right way, that they might go to a city of habitation. Oh that men would praise the Lord for His goodness, and His wonderful works to the children of men! For He satisfieth the longing soul, and filleth the hungry soul with goodness. (Ps. 107:1–9)

This has been literally fulfilled in me and mine. I praise the Lord Who has done great things for us. Hallelujah, Amen.

GLORIOUS NEW HOPE

THE MOST PRECIOUS TRUTH WHICH I have learnt since my conversion is the second coming of the Lord Jesus Christ. I firmly believe, as taught in the Bible, that the Lord Jesus Christ is coming soon. He will most certainly come and will not tarry. The signs of the times in the last decade have taught me to be waiting for Him. I was totally ignorant of this particular subject. It is not generally taught in this country. The missionaries connected with some denominations do not believe in it at all. They believe that Christ will come to judge the quick and the dead at the time of the last judgement, but they do not think He will come for His servants before the time of the resurrection of the dead and before the final judgement.

The hope of the appearing of our Saviour to take His redeemed ones to be with Him has been a great help to me in my Christian life. I praise the Lord for the great promise of His coming, and His counsel to watch and pray.

> Watch therefore: for ye know not
> what hour your Lord doth come.
> (Matt. 24:24)

Take ye heed, watch and pray;
for ye know not when the time is.
(Mark 13:33)

UNEXPECTED VISIT FROM THE GOVERNOR

ONE DAY DURING THIS MONTH, AS I was getting ready for my afternoon work, one of my fellow-workers came to the door of the office, followed by the Collector of Poona. Both told me that His Excellency the Governor of Bombay had come to visit Mukti. I was taken by surprise, for I never thought that the Governor would ever come to such an out-of-the-way place and visit an unpretending institution, which had not earned popularity by great achievements and by courting the favour of the great men of the country. In a few moments my surprise vanished, giving way to perfect pleasure at finding the Governor so simple and natural in his manner, though he was very dignified and grand.

It was delightful to see the greatest man of this presidency taking kindly notice of everyone who happened to come in his way, enquiring with interest of every little detail concerning the work. He seemed to be well acquainted with what was going on here. After inspecting all parts of the Mission, he bade us goodbye and went away. It was a very pleasant surprise, and we shall never forget his visit and kindness to us all.

UNEXPECTED VISIT FROM THE GOVERNOR

As we did not know about his visit, we had not made any preparations to receive him; so he saw us as we were; some walking about, some idly sitting where they were, some doing their work properly, some sweeping the ground and doing other housework, some dressed well and tidily, others in rags with unkempt hair, some giving themselves to their lessons and industry with diligence, and some just looking into the air doing nothing and thinking about nothing in particular.

It does one good to be taken by surprise in this way. The one great thought that filled my heart while the Governor was here, and after he went away, leaving a very pleasant impression on our mind, was that our Lord Jesus Christ is coming some day just in this manner, and those of us who are prepared to meet Him will have the joy of being caught up in the air to be with Him. How blessed it will be, not to have anything to be afraid of or anything that belongs to the enemy. How nice to be able to say with our Blessed Saviour, "The prince of this world cometh, and hath nothing in me" (John 14:30).

> The grace of God that bringeth salvation hath appeared to all men, teaching us that, denying ungodliness and worldly lusts, we should live soberly, righteously, and godly, in this present world; looking for that blessed hope, and the glorious appearing of the great God and our Saviour Jesus Christ; Who gave Himself for us, that He might redeem us from all iniquity, and purify unto Himself

a peculiar people, zealous of good works. (Titus 2:11–14)

A LOVING INVITATION

And take heed to yourselves, lest at any time your hearts be overcharged with surfeiting, and drunkenness, and cares of this life, and so that day come upon you unawares. For as a snare shall it come on all them that dwell on the face of the whole earth. Watch ye therefore, and pray alway, that ye may be accounted worthy to

> escape all these things that shall come to pass, and to stand before the Son of Man. (Luke 21:34–36)

If I were to write all that the Lord has done for me, even as much as it lies in my power to do so, the book would be too large for a person to read: so I have made the account of my spiritual experience as short as possible. I am very glad and very thankful to the Lord for making it possible for me to give this testimony of the Lord's goodness to me. My readers will scarcely realise the great spiritual needs of all my countrywomen and of my countrymen, too. The people of this land are steeped in sin and are sitting in a terrible darkness. May the Father of Light send them light and life by His chosen ones. We need witnesses for Christ and His great salvation freely

A LOVING INVITATION

offered to all men. Dear brother and sister, whoever may happen to read this testimony, may you realise your responsibility to give the gospel of Jesus Christ to my people in this land, and pray for them that they may each and all be cleansed from their filthiness and from all their idols, that they may find the true way of salvation.

My prayer for those readers who have not yet been saved is that they may seek and find Christ Jesus, our Blessed Redeemer, for the salvation of their souls.

> Our citizenship is in heaven, from whence also we wait for the Saviour, the Lord Jesus Christ. (Phil. 3:20)
>
> Unto Him that loved us, and washed us from our sins in His

own blood, And hath made us kings and priests unto God and His Father; to Him be glory and dominion for ever and ever. Amen. (Rev. 1:5–6)

March 1907

A NOTE FROM THE PUBLISHER

HOW DO WE ENTER INTO THE RELATIONSHIP with God through the Lord Jesus Christ about which Pandita Ramabai has told us? We need to understand that God truly loves us and desires that everyone come to know Him, the only true and holy God. But man is prevented from knowing God because of sin.

The Bible says that everyone has sinned, and that there is no one who is perfectly holy. God, however, requires holy and sinless people. Because of man's sin and God's holiness and love for us, Jesus Christ came to earth to die for our sins. Romans 5:8 says that because of our sin and the sacrifice of Jesus Christ on the cross, that Jesus Christ is God's only provision for man's sin. Jesus also said, "I am the way, the truth, and the life; no man cometh to the Father, but by me" (John 14:6).

You can receive Jesus Christ as your Savior by faith. Romans 6:23 says, "For the wages of sin is death; but the gift of God is eternal life through Jesus Christ our Lord." A way of expressing your faith is by praying a prayer such as the following:

> Lord Jesus, I need you. I know that I have done wrong in your sight. Thank you for dying on the cross

A NOTE FROM THE PUBLISHER

> for my sins. I now place my faith and trust in you as my Savior and Lord for the forgiveness of my sins.
>
> Thank you for forgiving my sins and for giving me eternal life. Take control of me, and make me what you want me to be. Amen.

You can pray that prayer right now to accept Jesus Christ as your personal Savior and Lord.

If you did pray that prayer and want more information, ask the one who gave you this booklet, or contact one of the following organizations:

Ramabai Mukti Mission
P.O. Box 4912, Clinton NJ 08809
muktimission.us
hopehealinglife@muktimission.us

Community Christian Ministries
P.O. Box 9754, Moscow ID 83843
www.ccmbooks.org
ccm@moscow.com
(208) 883–0997

www.ingramcontent.com/pod-product-compliance
Lightning Source LLC
Chambersburg PA
CBHW052156110526
44591CB00012B/1977